# Cyber Security Awareness for CEOs and Management

# Cyber Security Awareness for CEOs and Management

David Willson

Contributing Editor

Henry Dalziel

AMSTERDAM • BOSTON • HEIDELBERG • LONDON
NEW YORK • OXFORD • PARIS • SAN DIEGO
SAN FRANCISCO • SINGAPORE • SYDNEY • TOKYO

ELSEVIER

Syngress is an imprint of Elsevier

**SYNGRESS**

Syngress is an imprint of Elsevier
225 Wyman Street, Waltham, MA 02451, USA

**Notices**
Knowledge and best practice in this field are constantly changing. As new research and
experience broaden our understanding, changes in research methods or professional practices,
may become necessary.

Practitioners and researchers must always rely on their own experience and knowledge in
evaluating and using any information or methods described herein. In using such information
or methods they should be mindful of their own safety and the safety of others, including
parties for whom they have a professional responsibility.

To the fullest extent of the law, neither the Publisher nor the authors, contributors, or editors,
assume any liability for any injury and/or damage to persons or property as a matter of products
liability, negligence or otherwise, or from any use or operation of any methods, products,
instructions, or ideas contained in the material herein.

ISBN: 978-0-12-804754-5

**British Library Cataloguing-in-Publication Data**
A catalogue record for this book is available from the British Library

**Library of Congress Cataloging-in-Publication Data**
A catalog record for this book is available from the Library of Congress

For Information on all Syngress publications
visit our website at http://store.elsevier.com/Syngress

Working together
to grow libraries in
developing countries

www.elsevier.com • www.bookaid.org

# CONTENTS

# ABOUT THE CONTRIBUTING EDITOR

**Henry Dalziel** is a serial education entrepreneur, founder of Concise Ac Ltd, online cybersecurity blogger, and e-book author. He writes for the Concise-Courses.com blog and has developed numerous cybersecurity continuing education courses and books. Concise Ac Ltd develops and distributes continuing education content (books and courses) for cybersecurity professionals seeking skill enhancement and career advancement. The company was recently accepted onto the UK Trade & Investment's (UKTI) Global Entrepreneur Programme (GEP).

# INTRODUCTION

As a CEO, corporate executive or member of management are you concerned about cyber security, that inevitable data breach, how you will react, whether you will be sued or fired, and what you can do about it? This book provides an overview of the cyber threat/risks to your business and you or your position, and will discuss what you need to do, especially as CEOs, executives and management, to lower the risk, reduce or eliminate liability, and protect the reputation of the company, and yourself, as it relates to information security, data protection and data breaches.

Here's a little bit about my background: I grew up in New York. After attending law school I went on active duty with the U.S. Army. I spent 20 years in the Army as a JAG officer. During that time I engaged in a lot of trial work, prosecution and defense work. Halfway through my career I transitioned into operational and international law provided legal support for satellite operations and space control and then cyber operations, CNA, CND, and CNE, (computer network attack, defense and exploitation) providing legal advice on attacking, defending, and exploiting networks to defeat the enemy. During that time frame I was at the National Security Agency (NSA) and helped establish what is now called CYBERCOM. When I retired from the Army I started Titan Info Security Group. I'm a licensed attorney in New York, Connecticut, and Colorado. I hold the CISSP (Certification for Information System Security Professional). As the owner and sole practitioner of Titan Info Security Group I do risk management, risk assessments, security audits, policy and compliance work, incident response, management and oversight, support to law firms, hackback or active defense, and address all sorts of cyber and legal-related issues.

Here's the agenda. We'll cover how bad it is and should you be concerned—and I tell you, absolutely you need to be concerned—what the problem is as I see it, how data is lost and stolen, who the hackers are; it's important to know who's attacking you in order to defend yourself. What can you do to protect yourself and your business? And at the end we'll cover what are some of your fiduciary responsibilities and obligations as CEO or management, and so on and so forth.

Let's begin with two questions: First, will you or your company/firm be breached or hacked over the next year? And Second, will someone else or another firm be breached or hacked over the next year? Typically when I ask the first question only about 10% of the hands go up. But with the second question typically 80% to 90% of the hands go up. This begs the question, "why do you believe that your security is better than the guy next to you or some other company? Is your security better than the White House, the Pentagon, many large companies, Target, Sony, Home Depot, Scott Trade, the Office of Personnel Management (OPM), it goes on and on. So what is it about your security that you think makes you much better than everyone else?" The answer to that typically comes down to two arguments. Most do not really believe their security is better, but what they believe is that their company is too small for hackers to bother with, and, they don't have anything the hackers want. Throw those two theories out of the window. Face it, your company or firm will be breached. If it hasn't happened already, which is hard to believe, then it is just a matter of time. More likely is that you have been breached and don't even know it. Hackers want everything they can steal. Let's go ahead and look at the issues.

**David Willson**

# CHAPTER *1*

## How Bad Is It Out There?

Let's discuss about how bad it is, and whether or not you should be concerned. First of all, cyber threats, hacking and theft of data is much worse than most understand and would believe. So yes, you should be very concerned.

Here's a great analogy. As a gun owner, good safety dictates you assume and treat every gun as if it is loaded. The same applies to cyber security. Assume every network or computer device is or has been compromised in one way or another. I go through life assuming that my laptop and other computing devices have been compromised and there's nothing I can do about it. You have to make that assumption because unless you're a forensic examiner or malware analyst, can look at your computer logs daily and determine whether you have been infected or compromised, you can never be sure and it's better to be safe than sorry. If you assume you have been compromised you will be much more cautious with your data. With that in mind, preparation is the key. You must identify and attempt to lower risk, and take action to attempt to prevent a breach. But, as stated, preparation is the key. Prepare for that inevitable breach because it will happen.

### Breaches - Hacks

| In the Media | 2014 | 2015 |
|---|---|---|
| Target | 40 million credit card numbers | ------------------ |
| Home Depot | 56 million accounts | ------------------ |
| Sony | 25 gigs of sensitive employee data | ------------------ |
| OPM | Over 19 million impacted | ------------------ |
| Anthem | ------------------ | 80 million healthcare accts |
| AshleyMadison.com | ------------------ | Over 37 million impacted |
| YOU?? | Were you breached? | What could you lose? |

Let's review some recent major breaches. This is just a small sampling of what has appeared recently in the media. If you look at some of the websites that report data breaches, you'll see there're hundreds of businesses that are breached every month and sensitive information lost. Some of the major breaches most of us are familiar with include Target, 40 million credit card numbers; Home Depot, 56 million accounts; Sony, 25 gigs of sensitive employee information; Office of Personnel Management (OPM), this one is personal for me since I was in the military, 19 to 21 million, and the figure is likely much larger now. The latest news is that the OPM breach included the theft of fingerprints. With that number of records stolen, anyone who served in the military has to assume that their personal information was part of that breach. And it continues. Anthem Health, 80 million medical records stolen; Ashley Madison, 37 million, and not just names and social security numbers, but very personal information to include people being outed left and right as cheaters. So, where do you stand? Do you even know whether your business or firm has been breached? You need to assume you have been and plan from there. This attitude puts you in a much better perspective than saying to yourself, "I'm not worried, it won't happen to me." You're kidding yourself if you follow that line of thinking. The breaches are real and impacting all.

Later we will provide some more in depth discussion about the hackers, who they are, how they get in and the technology behind their techniques. Briefly though, the techniques of a hacker are not like those of someone breaking into a bank, your house, or shoplifting. Hackers use automated tools from the security of wherever their computer is, and operate virtually anonymously hopping from network to network to mask who they are and their location.

Imagine if someone was able to implant tools in retail stores or in banks all around the country, and at the press of a button these automated tools, like little robots, would begin stealing or shoplifting and tossing the merchandise into a device which then, like a pneumatic tube, transports the merchandise to wherever the thief desires. Usually to a storage space of some other unknowing warehouse owner. That is an attempt at a physical world analogy of the techniques utilized by hackers. Automated systems/software are used to compromise computers, home networks, business networks, etc. These compromised machines/networks are then used to target companies and other networks and steal and disrupt things. For instance, a botnet is a series of infected machines that are controlled by one or more hackers to compromise other machines and networks, send out phishing attacks, implement denial of service attacks, etc. Some of the largest botnets in the world consist of over a million infected computers and networks.

Let's consider the law of averages. How often does a hacker or attacker have to be right? Just once. How often do we, the defenders, defending our networks have to be right? One hundred percent of the time. It's 1% versus 100%. Those are some serious losing odds. Yet another reason why you should be so concerned. We are fighting a losing battle.

Before getting back to the hackers, let's look at another issue hindering companies. The IT companies and departments have been saddled with the job of security, and many do not have the budget, time, or even expertise to adequately do the job. Additionally, for most companies management treats cyber security as an IT/technical issue and therefore don't bother to pay attention and understand what is really going on. Now understand, my goal is not to pick on IT departments and IT people. They do a great job. But what is their focus? For most companies, it is uptime. Back in the day before cyber was a concern, the primary focus of IT was to install computers, setup the network, install software, get everything up and running, and make sure everyone is online and has 24/7 access. Today that is still the focus. Security is a distant second to that goal. Helpdesk support takes up much of the IT department's time. If you're using an outsourced IT company, security, in most cases, is really an afterthought, sort of an additional duty. The primary goal of many of these companies, based on what their clients requirements are, is to make sure the client is up and running. In order to be cost effective, most attempt to do this using automation to minimize the number of employees needed, as well as to limit the use of resources. The issue really becomes that of IT versus Suits. Suits want uptime, and IT knows it. Yes, management is concerned with and wants to know about threats, but most who do not have an IT background seem to treat the threats as sort of a theoretical or amorphous threat and fall prey to the attitude of, "I don't really think it will happen to me." Also, unfortunately, many IT support personnel, for a myriad of reasons, do not want to tell the leadership how bad the state of security is, how vulnerable the company really is, or how many attacks the company has actually suffered. The attitude appears to be, "I don't want to tell the emperor he has no clothes," "I don't want to tell everybody how vulnerable we really are because it makes me look bad, and makes me look like I'm not doing my job." In addition there are some IT personnel who believe they are the superman of all things technical and possess the attitude, "I can do it all" and, "nobody will ever get into my network." I've worked with a few of them or done assessments on a few of their companies, and typically it takes all of about 5 minutes to get in. Yes, five minutes. It is usually very simple, especially with that attitude.

The problem with some IT personnel believing they can do it all is that most are not cyber security experts, they are IT experts and the two jobs are not synonymous. For example, would you go to a podiatrist for back surgery, or a dermatologist for brain surgery? Similarly, you wouldn't hire your website designer to set up your network. So, don't assume your IT guy or Company is qualified to secure your network and data. Unfortunately this assumption is made a lot. I once worked with a big hospital in New York, the president told the IT guy, "Hey the HVAC (heating, ventilating and air) system is down. It's run by a computer. Go fix it. You're a computer guy." The IT guy looked at the president like he was crazy and said, "I don't know anything about HVAC systems." Don't make those assumptions. Don't assume your IT guy or your IT company is also a cyber security company unless they show that they have that expertise.

Moving on. Nobody truly knows how bad the threats and vulnerabilities are until you have that sort of nuclear event in the company when all explodes and everyone is scrambling to figure out what happened and how to react. You must be prepared. It's coming.

The more classes and lectures I give and the more assessments I do, the more I realize that many people don't understand the dynamics behind cyber security. First of all, there is no silver bullet. There is no piece of hardware, no piece of software, no process or procedure that's going to keep you secure. Security is a process, and that process must be managed. First you must identify and understand the risk, threats, and vulnerabilities. As stated above, IT does not equal security. IT ensures your equipment is set up and running and continues to run efficiently, e.g., uptime. Security is completely separate. Security utilizes technology, but the technology is just a tool. You must also understand how the vulnerabilities are created by understanding the behaviors of the users, how the data is collected, processed, stored, and utilized, along with other factors. Currently, the end-user is likely to be the greatest vulnerability and threat to your data. Technology can help lower the end user risk, but training plays a much larger role in reducing that threat and vulnerability. Understanding and protecting the data is why current advice recommends that companies appoint a Chief Information Officer (CIO), and/or a risk manager. Obviously, these roles will depend on the size of the company, budget, and other factors, but at a minimum, one or more can be assigned as extra duties.

www.youngupstarts.com

# Compliance $\neq$

http://www.bmibank.com

While we are on the topic of what does and does not equal security, you need to understand that compliance, such as HIPAA/HITECH, SOX, GLBA, PCI, etc., does not equal security. Just because your company is HIPAA compliant or PCI compliant does not mean you're secure. For example, HIPAA requires a password. But, one, two, three, four is not a good password. So you may be compliant with the password requirement, but that doesn't mean you're secure.

## Where is the weakest link in the chain?

# The End User!

# You are the weakest link!

So what or who is the weakest link in the chain? As stated above, we are, the end users, the people behind the computers on the keyboards. We are the weakest link because of our behaviors and actions.

We click on everything, open everything. It is our actions and behaviors with regard to technology that allows the compromise to the network and to our most sensitive data in most cases. Yes, there are still vulnerabilities and weaknesses in the network hackers attempt to exploit, but the end user is probably one of the easiest ways to get in.

Consider this quote from an Experian Data Breach survey: "Survey results show that a data breach is often the result of human error or a crime—neither of which can be 100 percent prevented. As such, companies must put measures in place—training, preparedness plans, guidelines, etc.—to help protect their customers' information." As stated above, training, preparedness plans, guidelines, incident response, data breach plans, business continuity, disaster recovery; it's all a process. You can't simply put a security program together and forget it. Security is not a set and forget concept. Put the plans in place and then exercise them and make sure everybody knows and understands their role.

The million dollar question then is, what constitutes good or reasonable security? Currently no set standard exists as the gold standard for good security which will ensure you company will not be breached and thus sued. The best you can do is implement a process and manage that process. You security should be based on your budget, the information you collect, and the resources available at the time and a risk assessment. You must be able to show due diligence in implementing and managing your security program. You must be able to declare, "I implemented reasonable security and managed it." That way, when everything hits the fan, you can confidently claim that you did A, B, and C to try and protect information; that was the best you could do. That should be the goal: implement reasonable security and manage it. Don't look for a standard to make you secure. Standards are good as guidance —and many provide a decent base for setting up and implementing a program, but there is no one standard that's going to achieve the reasonable security goal all by itself. A little later we will discuss this concept more.

# CHAPTER 2

# How Is Data Stolen?

Now, let's discuss how data is lost and stolen. Focusing on the end user as the greatest vulnerability, the three main avenues hackers use and that cause data to be lost or stolen are email, Internet, and social media. I say lost or stolen because in many cases data is lost due to our own negligence and mistakes, e.g. lost phones, mobile devices, etc.

First, clicking is probably one of your worst enemies. When we received email and it contains a link or an attachment, most of us will click the link in the mail or click on and download the attachment without even a second thought. Worse yet, most of us have pictures and Internet enabled links activated so when we open an email the pictures appear as well as Internet images. These pictures and images could potentially be downloading malware or viruses to your computer without your knowledge. First tip, your email should be set up so that pictures and Internet or HTML text does not load automatically but you have to actively request to load them. This book is not long enough to walk you through how to do this but, ask your IT person or search on "How to protect or secure email" on the Internet.

Another avenue hackers utilize to steal data is the Internet. We do a lot of Internet searches using Google or other search browsers. Hackers either attempt to trick us into going to fake websites or seed legitimate websites with malware or viruses. For instance, you click a link in an email believing it is taking you to a legitimate website, but in reality it is a fake site made to look like the real one. Maybe a banking site. Once there, you insert your username and password and either the site forwards you to the real site or you get a 404 error. Either way the hackers now have your username and password. Similarly, as you click around legitimate sites you could be unknowingly downloading malware or viruses that have been inserted by hackers who breached the website. So, beware. In many cases this type of malware and viruses would be very difficult to detect and defeat. But if you keep it in the back of your mind that it exists, and if your Spidey sense alarms as you're clicking through websites, then get out of it and move on. Paranoia, in the context of technology, is probably a very good thing. Just remember, clicking can get you in hot water, so caution and a touch of paranoia are good.

This is not to say you can never click the links in emails. I do frequently if I trust the email and the sender. If you know you can trust it, then fine. For most of us we get a lot of emails every day and quickly flip through them, in fact blast through them. It can be exciting to see a clip, picture, or video someone sent, or see if you have a potential customer. Someone may send you an email with a link claiming, "Check this out." It could be from somebody legitimate or could be a fake. So, you open and download it or you click the link and boom, you've been compromised and not even know it. Many of us are also very distracted as we email. An extreme example is when I see people on the highway, zipping down the road at 60 miles an hour looking at text messages and emails. First of all, it's extremely dangerous and second you're clicking on things not even really paying attention to it because you're supposed to have your eyes on the road. So every click is a potential virus, malware, and/ or message stating you've been hacked or breached. Obviously you're not going to get a message saying you've been hacked or breached, but that's the end result.

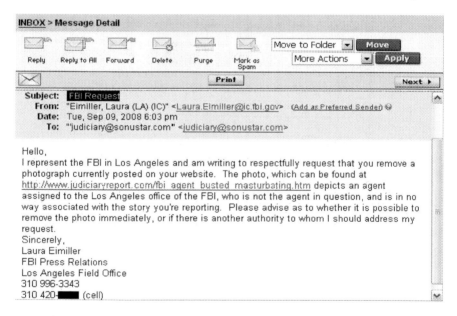

Let's review some phishing attack emails. This first one is supposed to make you believe it is from the FBI. When you get an email from someone you do not recognize, the first thing you should look for is whether it looks suspicious and how many misspellings you see. The reason for this is that many phishing emails come from overseas where English is not their first language, and, in many cases, they don't bother with spell check. Trust your gut if it tells you something does not look right. In this email, the email address scheme looks correct, it includes IC for intelligence community as well as FBI.gov which appears correct. But the email address: judiciary@sonustar.com gives me a little pause and should cause your Spidey sense to go up. This is obviously a fake email based on the way it's written. These types of emails, from organizations like the FBI, are meant to be a scare technique to get you to click the link in the email quickly out of fear or concern. As stated, stop, take a breath and investigate a little. There is no reason why the FBI would be contacting you. If the FBI was looking for you, more than likely they would knock on your door, or kick it in. Anyway, don't click on the link. If you really need to know, this email includes a phone number, you can call, or you can contact your local FBI office or even their website to investigate more about the email. You could also see if this Laura person, allegedly an agent, answers if you call the mobile number. You might even Google this type of message and see if there's a scam out there. When I receive suspicious emails I check the Internet for the particular scam. Another investigation technique would be to type the URL www.judiciaryreport.com/fbi into your browser and see what pops up. But the bottom line is, you just need to be cautious.

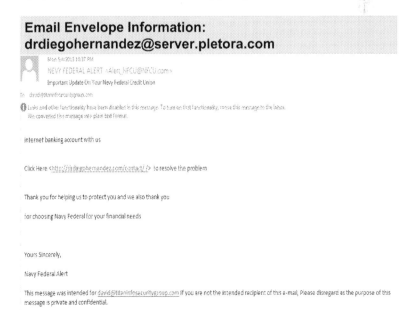

**Email Envelope Information:**
**drdiegohernandez@server.pletora.com**

Mon 5/4/2015 10:37 PM

NEVY FEDERAL ALERT <Alert_NFCU@NFCU.com>

Important Update On Your Navy Federal Credit Union

To    david@titaninfosecuritygroup.com

Links and other functionality have been disabled in this message. To turn on that functionality, move this message to the Inbox.
We converted this message into plain text format.

Internet banking account with us

Click Here <http://drdiegohernandez.com/contact/ /> to resolve the problem

Thank you for helping us to protect you and we also thank you

for choosing Navy Federal for your financial needs

Yours Sincerely,

Navy Federal Alert

This message was intended for david@titaninfosecuritygroup.com If you are not the intended recipient of this e-mail, Please disregard as the purpose of this message is private and confidential.

This next email appears to come from the Navy Federal Credit Union. If you look at the top of the email you'll see it says Nevy Federal Alert, Navy spelled with an "E." This is your first clue that this is probably not a legitimate email. I can tell you that all of the banks that I've spoken with stated that they do not send emails to customers as a generic email. They always include the customer's name. This email was sent to me as is evident from my email addresses on the "To" line. Similar to the last email there's a link the hackers, or phishing attackers or scammers, want you to click on. Another red flag is the link. Why would a navy federal credit union want me to click on the link that says: drdiegohernandez.com/contact? This is obviously a huge red flag. Do not click the link. Finally, when you look at the envelope information or the metadata in the properties of the email it reveals where the email actually came from. It was not from the credit union.

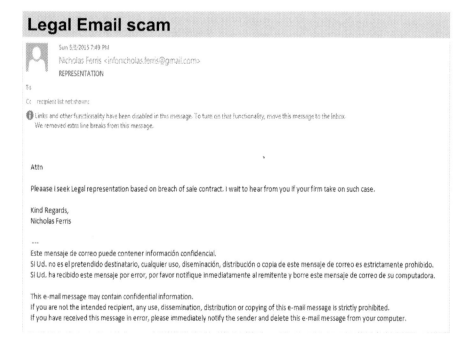

This next email is a typical legal scam. The scammers are seeking to scam attorneys, typically into laundering money for them. Look at the header information and you will see that no name or email address is listed in the "To" line. The only data shown is "recipients list not shown" on the "CC" line. The "From" line indicates infonicholas. ferris@gmail.com sent the email from a Gmail account. Also, a close look of the body of the email reveals very poor English: "Please I seek legal representation." Additionally no contact information exists, there's nothing to click on and nothing to download. In this case, the scammers are hoping you will respond back via email, agree to take the case and ask for a retainer of $XXX.XX amount. The scammers will then send you the retainer and likely a short time later will notify you that they decided not to pursue the case and ask you to please send the retainer back minus your fee. When you do this, basically what you've done is laundered money for these people. There are other types of scams along this line. So, be very cautious of this, especially attorneys.

Sun 5/3/2015 5:00 PM

Wells Fargo Online <Wellsfargo@secureserver.com>

Unauthorized activity on your online account

To   david@startinsecuritygroup.com

Links and other functionality have been disabled in this message. To turn on that functionality, move this message to the Inbox.
The Outlook Junk Email filter marked this message as spam.
Outlook blocked access to the following potentially unsafe attachments: Validation Form.html.

Dear Wells Fargo customer,

We have recently detected that a different computer user has attempted gaining access to your online account and multiple passwords were attempted with your user ID.

It is necessary to re-confirm your account information and complete a profile update.

You can do this by downloading the attached file and updating the necessary fields.

Note: If this process is not completed within 24-48 hours we will be forced to suspend your account online access as it may have been used for fraudulent purposes.

Completion of this update will avoid any possible problems with your account.

Thank you for being a valued customer.

(C) 2015 Wells Fargo. All rights reserved.

This next email appears to come from Wells Fargo. Similar to the Navy Credit Union email above, in this one, no customer name appears. For me a huge red flag is the fact that I do not bank with Wells Fargo. Unlike the emails we have looked at so far, in this email the scammers are looking for recipients to click on the attachment rather than a link. As it states, "You can do this by downloading the attached file and updating necessary fields." When I created the image of the email the attachment that was with the email didn't show on the copy, but there was an attachment with this email. Just as you should not click on a link, you should certainly not click on the attachment. Obviously it's a scam. As stated above, look for misspellings, improper English, or things that just don't seem right. If you are really concerned about something like this, call the bank and ask them about it.

Wed 5/6/2015 2:07 AM

Holly Twomey <kj@worksmartllc.com>

from: Holly Twomey

To    Erin Clare Sears; dan conners; John Cook; kathy cooper; Vakita O SK2 NOSC Gulfport MS Crawford; Csouza; dana dzel; danaparelkatz; david; david; ddeker; debra veasy; April Decaillo; deltastrike; deltastrike; Denise Fraguzzi; Jerry Dennis; dennispcallanan; iffority; Jackie eaton

Links and other functionality have been disabled in this message. To turn on that functionality, move this message to the Inbox.
The Outlook Junk Email filter marked this message as spam.
We converted this message into plain text format.


Hi! How are you?


Have you seen this http://supremefire.com.au/town.php before? Oprah had been using it for over a year!
Holly Twomey


Sent from Yahoo Mail for iPhone <https://yho.com/footer0>

In this image we will look at how you can explore deeper and research the IP address from where the email was sent to provide clues as to its legitimacy. First, you need to know that email addresses can be spoofed. Let's say, through some investigation, either via your website or searching social media, I determined your name and/or email address. I can then send an email to whoever my target is and make it look like it's coming from you. When you look behind that email address at the properties, the envelope header or the metadata, you can see the actual IP address from where that email was sent. For instance, this email says it's from Holley Twomey, with an email address of: kj@worksmartllc.com. The first red flag is that the name and email address do not appear to match. Second, when you go to the worksmartllc.com website it has nothing to do with what this email or this person seems to be talking about. It's possible that the Worksmartllc website was compromised or their email server was compromised and someone is using the server to send out scam or phishing emails. Also, like many of the others emails we have reviewed, there is a link the scammers want you to click on. Again, don't do it. Also, random names appear in this email as recipients, none of which make sense. The fact that you do not know the person should raise at least a small red flag. If you were really interested in Oprah and what this was about you could simply Google it, but don't click the link. In the alternative you could type the URL into your browser to see where it takes you. Be cautious about this as well since hacker sites, fake but legitimate looking sites, can create problems for you as well. Finally, another technique

I have used if the URL is too long is to right-click the link, copy, paste it into a Word document so that anything unseen behind it is stripped out. You can then copy the URL from the Word document and paste it into your browser to see what comes up.

Similar to the fake emails that can be created, fake web links can be created. For instance, as a hacker if you want get people to go to your hacker site, www.mymalwaresite.com, but are concerned no one will click it out of fear of contracting a malware or virus, you can disguise the URL to say whatever you want. You can change the name of the URL to something like www.freemoney.com, but when your victims click this link they will actually be taken to www.mymalwaresite.com.

Fri 5/1/2015 1:02 PM

Usaa <Usecurity@usaa.com>

Important Message From Usaa

To    Recipients

Links and other functionality have been disabled in this message. To turn on that functionality, move this message to the Inbox.
The Outlook Junk Email filter marked this message as spam.
We removed extra line breaks from this message.
We converted this message into plain text format.

Dear Usaa Customer,

Your online banking account has been suspended
(Reason: Violation of Terms Of Service)

Update and Restore your online account as soon as possible

For your protection, you must verify this activity before you can continue using your account.

kindly CLICK HERE <http://bolivspine.com/wp-includes/images/wiw/w8.html> to review your account activity.

Copyright USAA Online Banking All Rights Reserved.

Thank you for using usaa.com.

Copyright ? 2015 USAA.

### Received: from tx3-csb2.smtp.ucla.edu ([169.232.46.189])

This next email appears to be from USAA, and is another bank email. Many phishing attacks appear to come from banks. As you can see, this one, like others, is sent to unknown recipients and does not address a named individual, but states, "Dear USAA customer." This is your first alert. Also, the S and two A's are in small caps, which should cause more suspicion. Again, similar to others, the scammers want you to click on the link. Also, as stated with the FBI email, in many of these phishing attacks, it's all about urgency. The scammers want you to do something quickly and that's how they're trying to trip you up. Obviously in this email it states, "Your online banking account has been suspended." As you look closer, the link they want you to click reads, bolivspine.com/wp, which is normally a Word Press site. At the bottom of the email you can see I have written the actual address the email came from as well as the IP address: "Received from. tx3-csb2.smtp.ucla.edu ([169.232.46.189]" This is not a typical IP address for a banking site. This is a typical internal IP address for a company network, which is not where emails are sent from. If you do a "Whois" look up on the IP address it reveals that the IP address comes from the University of California Los Angeles. So it appears as though this email was sent from an IP address belonging to UCLA. The likelihood in this case is that UCLA's server has been hacked and is being used to send spam and phishing attacks.

| IP Locator & IP Lookup Basic Tracking Info | |
|---|---|
| IP Address: | 169.232.46.189 |
| Reverse DNS: | 189.46.232.169.in-addr.arpa |
| Hostname: | tx3-csb2.smtp.ucla.edu |
| Nameservers: | ns3.dns.ucla.edu >> 192.35.210.7<br>ns2.dns.ucla.edu >> 192.12.234.140<br>ns1.dns.ucla.edu >> 192.35.225.7<br>ns4.dns.ucla.edu >> 128.171.28.220 |
| IP Blacklist Check: | Not Blacklisted |
| IP Lookup Location For IP Address: 169.232.46.189 | |
| Continent: | North America (NA) |
| Country: | United States ▦ (US) |
| Capital: | Washington |
| State: | California |
| City Location: | Los Angeles |
| Postal: | 90095 |
| Area: | 310 |
| Metro: | 803 |
| ISP: | University of California - Office of the President |
| Organization: | University of California, Los Angeles |
| AS Number: | AS52 University of California, Los Angeles |

This next image is a screenshot of the Whois lookup of the IP address. Again, you can find the IP address by looking at the properties of the email. If you use Outlook for email, merely open the email message, click on file and go to properties. Look for the IP address which was, like I said, 169.232.46.189. The fact that the UCLA server came up is not unusual simply because a lot of universities are breached due to limited security and since they keep their networks relatively open to allow students access to email and servers for studying and such.

Since we are discussing scams there is one you should know about that is costing companies a lot of money. The FBI continuously warns about this scam. Hackers somehow determine the email address of the CEO or other executive of a company. They also determine who in the company is responsible for money transfers and the types of transfers the company typically engages in. The hackers then send an email that appears to come from the CEO or other executive of a company to someone who handles money transfers. The email, as stated above, is worded to instill a sense of urgency in the recipient. The email demands that a certain amount be transferred to a specific account overseas quickly. Unfortunately many companies are falling for this scam. One method of defeating this is to put processes in place requiring confirmation and/or double checks prior to any transfer. At a minimum the recipient of the email should phone or text the CEO or executive to verify the legitimacy of the request. Emailing may be a concern since the hackers may have access to or co-opted the company email server and any email sent to the CEO could be going directly to the hackers. This is why an alternate means of communication should be chosen. Some of these scams are very sophisticated. The hackers were able to collect intelligence about the CEO, knowing when the CEO is out of town, they know the company email scheme, and they know the company's procedures for conducting money transfers. A lot of this data is available via social media, but other social engineering techniques were likely used.

Dear Capital One TowerNet[SM] or Treasury Optimizer user,

As part of the new terms and conditions of the Data Access Agreement between your organization and the Capital One, your organization will be given a Digital Certificate.

Because of the private nature of the client data, worldwide access via Web to that data, and the potential for fraud, the system must be certain of user identity and authorization. Capital One online banking services use two security mechanisms:
1. Customer & User Codes and passwords to identify users; and
2. Digital certificates to ensure that the user is access the business services through a valid computer, in a trusted organization.

Each registered user must have the Capital One's digital certificate installed on his or her machine in order to access online banking services.

To pickup and install your Digital Certificate, please visit:

http://towernet.capitalonebank.com/capitaloneid/usersdir/formpage.asp?index.php?em=henne@lists.mindspring.com&id=919051171332075579701526958 0158

Yet another bank email. This one appears to have come from Capital One. The real point here, like many others is that the scammers want you to click the link. As mentioned above, if you have to type it in or do a right-click copy, then do so to see what it is. Unless you are an expert with IP address and URL schemes, you likely do not know what MindSpring is in the URL, neither do you know what all those numbers are in the URL, or all those other characters. Also, the link towernet.capitalone does not sound legitimate.

## Apply Online

*Dear Valued Customer :*

As part of our security measures, we regularly screen activity in the Bank of America Online Banking system. We recently contacted you after noticing an issue on your account. We requested information from you for the following reason:

Our system requires further account verification.

To restore your account, please Sign in to Online Banking.

Please Note:
If we do no receive the appropriate account verification within 48 hours, then we will assume this Bank account is fraudulent and will be suspended. The purpose of this verification is to ensure that your bank account has not been fraudulently used and to combat the fraud from our community.

Finally an email appearing to come from Bank of America, with a definite sense of urgency. It requests that the account be verified within 48 hours, and asks you to click the link. Certainly if you never opened an account or you don't even bank with Bank of America you shouldn't be clicking on this.

Finally, I recently received an email that stated that the money transfer had been completed for $12,000. I did not recognize the sender and it provided no information other than the statement above, a transfer number, and stated that in order to see more details I should open the attached Word document. As you might imagine, I did not open the attachment and deleted the email. No one gratuitously sends me money.

Let's take a quick look at how hackers obtain a lot of their intelligence about their targets, us. Most people are active on more than one social media site. We post things and get constant updates and requests to connect. And so we want to click, click, click, and post, post, post.

*"Nearly every day consumers willingly provide their personal information to organizations online with no hesitation, neglecting to realize how that information can be exposed due to employee negligence, insider maliciousness, system glitches or attacks by cyber criminals."*[1]

This is from an Experian data breach and Ponemon Institute study. But in addition to what is stated here, most of us constantly put a lot of data out on Facebook and other social media. A great example from many years ago, is the guy from Massachusetts who bought a big screen TV and then took a picture of it. Most phone cameras at that time, and some still today, would embed the latitude and longitude, e.g. location, of where the picture was taken on the photo. In this case hackers were able to determine where the guy lived. This genius then posted that he was going on a vacation to the Bahamas and would be gone for a week. While he was on vacation, hackers or burglars who saw his Facebook posts, went to his house and stole his TV. The lesson learned is that we put way too much information out there and it makes it easy for hackers to use social engineering and cyber intelligence to figure out who we are and how best to target us.

[1]"Is Your Company Ready for a Big Data Breach? The Second Annual Study on Data Breach Preparedness," Ponemon Institute, Sponsored by Experian Data Breach Research (2014).

Again, never, never ever click on links and emails. If you have a LinkedIn account likely have received many connection requests, or friend requests from Facebook. Rather than clicking the link, go to the site. Type in www.LinkedIn.com and then login or type in the URL for Facebook. The problem with clicking the link is that it could be false. I've received connection requests from LinkedIn and when I logged into LinkedIn that request was not there. Similar to the scam or phishing emails the hackers are hoping you will click the link in the request believing you are logging into the actual LinkedIn site. As we discussed above, the same applies to your bank. You should always type the bank name into the browser and then log in. This is very important, don't click the link in the email for your bank.

Another good tip is you should try and avoid banking on smart-phones and mobile devices. It's just not that secure right now. Use your computer or laptop, but even with this be careful. If you're going to your bank online with a computer or laptop, close everything, all windows. Close your email and all other browsers. Don't have Facebook other social media, various searches open, etc. as well as your email. Close everything and then open a browser and type in the URL for the bank. This is a more secure way of banking. It's not the most secure way, but it is a more secure way.

If you go to krebsonsecurity.com, Brian offers a post wherein he explains how to set up a bootable CD or a thumb drive that will allow you to be even more secure when banking or working with financial transactions. Additionally, if your bank and any other service that requires a login offers two factor authentication you should take advantage of it. Two factor authentication consists of a username and password, which is one factor, and then usually a one-time pin, typically sent via text message. This, for the most part, ensures that if a hacker is able to guess or determine your username and password, he will not be able to access your account unless he has access to your text or sms messages.

Finally, ensure you keep all your systems up to date with security updates. First, you will never get a security update through your email. These updates pop up or appear on your computer automatically if you have this function enabled to load automatically. Do not click on links that pretend to be security updates. Also, if you're surfing the

Internet and a window pops reading "You've been compromised. Click here to clean your computer," don't do it.

Here's another problem. We all enjoy the convenience of technology. We want to be connected 24/7. In this quest for convenience we reject long, complicated passwords that have to be changed every so often. This leads to easy passwords that we can remember and then use the same on all accounts. If a hacker steals or guesses your password, and like many people, you use that same password for multiple logins, that hacker now has access to all of those accounts, banking, social media, email, etc.

## *The Tools/Toys/Communication*

Let's talk about mobility or mobile devices. Here are some of the devices we use, some are a little outdated. Many of us feel disconnected without all of these devices, yet, we lay them down, leave them in airports, in hotels, and multiple other places. How often have you heard someone say or you said yourself, "I can't find my phone?" I have found many phones in airports on chairs, at gates, and places like that. None of these devices were password protected. I was at the airport one day and sitting on a chair at the gate and saw a mobile phone that someone had left. While asking who might have lost it, someone said, "Oh well just look at the last number called." Lo and behold it wasn't password protected. When I opened it the first number that came up said, "My wife." So I gave the phone to the gate agents.

A recent Trend Micro report states that 41% of all breaches are due to lost mobile devices. As stated above, we leave devices everywhere and they are not password protected.[2] My hope is by the end of this book all of your mobile devices should be password protected. Certainly if they are company devices, and absolutely if they are personal devices, protect, protect, protect.

www.dreamatico.com

# The Castle Walls
# have Fallen!

Let's address the next problem or issue. In the past we could protect all sensitive data and equipment by keeping it behind walls, secure it, lock it down, and put locks on it. Unfortunately the castle walls have fallen primarily due to all of the mobile devices just shown. What we have now is a massive amount of connected devices and networks where data flows instantaneously around the world. Think about all of your current connections. Not just who you communicate with on a daily basis, but all of the support behind those communications, like the ISP, those companies running the servers for your email, texts, social media, as well as who maintains your networks, who has access to your data, etc. Consider the IT support, cloud providers, and many other connections and access.

---

[2]"Follow the Data: Dissecting Data Breaches and Debunking Myths Trend Micro Analysis of Privacy Rights Clearinghouse 2005–2015 Data Breach Records," Trend Micro (2015)

# Who are You Connected To?

You may believe your connections look like this, and maybe even larger than this. Our data is everywhere so we have to take a concerted effort to determine, "Where is that data and how am I best protecting it?" Rather than just taking technology for granted and assuming there is nothing to worry about, we have to be very careful about this information and how we're securing and what we do with it.

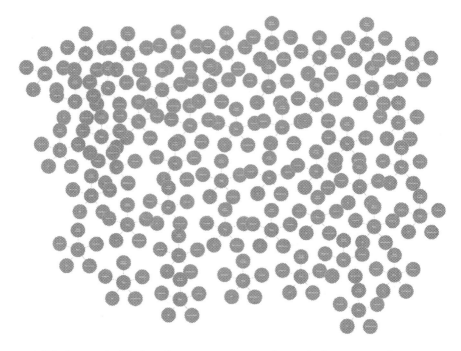

This image is likely a better representation of what most of our connections look like. The data is everywhere, so we must be more diligent about how we are managing and securing this information.

# CHAPTER 3

## Who Are the Hackers?

Let's discuss who the hackers are. This is important because if you understand who's coming after you or who's trying to attack you or steal your data then you have a better chance of trying to protect it.

So who are the hackers? What are they looking for? I'll tell you right now, they're looking for everything. I hear a lot of businesses say, "Oh I don't worry about it. I'm too small. They wouldn't want anything I have. I don't have anything the hackers want." Trust me. They want everything: email addresses, phone numbers, names, sensitive information, trade secrets, everything and anything they can steal. Certainly the information that you don't think is of any value has value for spammers seeking to send out all kinds of spam email ads such as the Canadian meds or the Viagra email spam many of us get. Also, what are the hackers' tools and how do they get in? We've spent some time on how they get in; typically phishing emails, as you click around on links, social media, and other techniques, but we will cover a little bit more.

## Who is Attacking/Who are the Hackers?

gizmodo.com

www.telegraph.co.uk

www.welivesecurity.com

donsurber.blogspot.com

rt.com

Who are they? The teenage kid trying to prove himself, sort of the introvert in the basement, still exists and can cause some headaches. The next group consists of the numerous hacker groups like Anonymous that you can see in the picture with the mask. Those are the groups that are looking to send messages, make a political point and steal money. Then there is, on the far right, the wise guys, organized crime. Hacking has gotten so profitable that a lot of organized crime syndicates have moved away from gambling, drugs and prostitution and moved into hacking because it's a lot lower risk and a lot higher profit. Next, you have the nation states like Russia, China, and others that are going after military and trade secrets. It appears from articles and reports that from the west, primarily the Chinese, nation-states are trying to steal secrets, both company and military. In contrast when you look east nations like Russia and others, as well as the hackers there, are trying to steal money. Sure, there is a quest for military and corporate secrets, but more theft. In the lower middle you see the terrorist groups. The Syrian Electronic Army (SEA), ISIS and ISIS supporters, Al Qaeda, and other terrorist groups that are hacking for money, to recruit, to send messages, steal intelligence, etc. Finally you have the typical criminal seeking to steal money or send out spam. As we become more and more connected the numbers of hackers increases. When you can hide behind a keyboard and attack someone or a network from the other side of the world, the risk appears very low. Compare that to the risk of putting on a mask, grabbing a gun and running into a bank to rob it.

Hacker's List | Find a professional hacker | Home
https://**hackerslist**.com/ ▾
Hiring a hacker shouldn't be a difficult process, we believe that finding a trustworthy professional hacker for hire should be a worry free and painless experience.
Projects  - Find Hackers  - Favorite  - How It Works

Hire a hacker
**hirenhack**.com/ ▾
Hirenhack.com Hire a Hacker is a professional hacker team can help you hack email account,change university grades, hack Facebook account, Ddos websites, ...

Hacker for Hire Reviews - before you hire a hacker read ...
**hackerforhirereview**.com/ ▾
Been Scammed by a hacker for hire Reviews about hacker for hire services.

How To Hire A Hacker — It's easier than you might think | BGR
bgr.com/2015/01/16/how-to-**hire-a-hacker**/ ▾  Boy Genius Report ▾
Jan 16, 2015 - Most Internet users are scared of hackers, and rightfully so. While the terms is sometimes used to describe any computer programmer, ...

Hacker For Hire Online
neighborhood**hacker**.com/ ▾
Hacker for hire services. Hire a hacker and let us Hack your Hacker! Professional online hacker for hire.

HIRE THE HACKER - HACKERS FOR HIRE - Hire ...
**hirethehacker**.com/ ▾
hire the hacker , hackers for grade changes , email hackers , facebook hackers , hackers for hire , hacking for cheap prices ,ethical hackers for hiring .

Hire a hacker
www.**hacker**1337.com/ ▾
hire a hacker online that is professionall Email password hacking, facebook hacker

When you Google the term "hackers" here's, what pops up. This is a screenshot of what you'll find: "hacker for hire," "hacker for hire reviews," "how to hire a hacker," etc. Now granted, a lot of these ads are to assist people having online problems who are seeking help. Some of them though, are real hackers, or should I say computer experts who are comfortable delving into the gray area of the law and beyond. I know people who are actual hackers that you can hire. They will go after someone else causing you problems online. Some of these hackers are legitimate requiring you sign a contract explaining what they will and will not do, like violate the law. Some of them though, you pay the money and they'll do whatever you want. It's that easy.

For those seeking to be hackers, it is also very easy. There are numerous books available, and if you don't have the skill to build your own tools you can easily get the software online for sale. There is an entire underground or dark web with hacker sites that offers hackers for hire, hacker tools, malware and viruses for sale, and the use of or lease of hacker tools. There is even hacker IT help support to set up and maintain the malicious software. Finally, you can also pay for an online subscription to keep the software up and running and receive updates to your hacker software. Very little skill is involved. This is not to say that all hackers have no skill. There are some extremely talented hackers out there. That's what makes this all really scary. On the flip side, there are some very talented good guys, but the odds are against the good guys. It is much more difficult to defend than it is to attack.

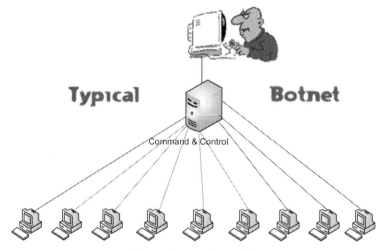

http://ubuntubook.wordpress.com/2011/06/11/construyendo-un-botnet/

This above image is an example of one of the schemes hackers use to infect, attack, exploit vulnerabilities and send spam. This is called a botnet. Think of a botnet as an inverted pyramid. The hacker is at the tip. He uses his computer to attack and exploit one computer infecting and compromising it. He then uses the compromised machine to infect others. Like the old adage goes, he tells two friends and they tell two friends and they tell two friends and they tell two friends until you have this whole web of infected machines that are being controlled by that one person, the hacker. Some of the largest botnets in the world are a million or more infected computers and servers. These computers are your home computer, your business servers, sometimes mobile devices, etc. Most people whose computer or network are infected don't even know it. That's why I stated earlier I go through life assuming that my electronics have been compromised and I may not know it, nor is there a lot I can do about it. Chances are you've probably been breached and compromised and don't even know it either. Also, just because your computer or server is compromised does not necessarily mean hackers are stealing anything from you. They could be just using your server or computer to attack other people or infect other machines, or to store the proceeds of their nefarious activities.

Consider home security as an analogy. If a burglar really wants to get into your house, do you think he can? Obviously yes. If he were to sit outside your home or frequently drive through the neighborhood, he could figure out when you're home, when you're not, what type of alarm system you have, whether you have a dog, whether you have weapons, whether there are open windows at any given time. He may even use sites like Zillow to research your home layout, and social media to learn what type of person you are and maybe how many people live there. Is your neighborhood noisy, with lots of traffic, barking dogs, kids playing, or a secluded enough area that he could just break a window hidden by shrubbery and get in? There are many factors. If he wants to sit there and take as much time as he needs to collect intelligence, like a lot of hackers, especially nation-state hackers, he could learn all he needed.

The true professionals, based on the time they have will usually go in low and slow, take their time, sometimes months or years, to get in and then sit quietly and then slowly siphon stuff out. Bottom line, if the hackers want in, they will get in and there's not a whole lot you can do about it.

# CHAPTER 4

# How to Protect Your Business

Let's discuss what you can do to protect your business and yourself.

## You a gambling man?

## No? Then Protect Yourself!

Okay, if you're a gambling man then don't do anything. Don't protect yourself. But if not, then you need a plan. You need to protect yourself.

Here are three steps I provide to business owners: first, determine the information you collect, process, and store, and how it is secured; understand where that information is and who has access to it, e.g., your IT provider, your cloud provider; is your data in the cloud?, on mobile devices, and where are those mobile devices, who has control over them; etc.? Second, draft or have the proper policies drafted and reviewed, to include a security policy, acceptable use, social media, incident response, etc. If you are subject to compliance regulations, like healthcare or financial, then you need to make sure your policies reflect what you are doing to secure that information and deal with the privacy issues. Third, training, training, and training. Everybody needs to be trained on the policies as well as cyber threats. Training, similar to this book is necessary to explain how information is lost, stolen, who the hackers are, the information they're looking for, and how to protect it.

In the next few pages we will discus tips you can use to improve your security:

First of all, have you turned off default passwords? For instance, servers and firewalls come with default passwords that are either not turned on, or the default is in use. Hackers are able to get the default passwords because at one point in time manufacturers, and possibly still today, some manufacturers put default passwords on the Internet to make it easier to access, set up and repair devices. Hackers are still able to get the passwords and gain access to hardware devices.

Next, are you using antivirus or anti-malware software? Make sure it's updated and in use.

Have you hired a IT company to set up your network and make it secure? If so you hired you are secure, right? Is the IT company you hired secure? Have you asked them? Ask them if they are secure and how they keep data secure? Ask them when the last time was, if ever, they had a security audit? Don't trust your sensitive data to people or companies unless you know their level of security.

Okay, now let's talk about some good practices to follow:

– I mentioned earlier that you need to lock all of your mobile devices. If they are lost or stolen you will have less to worry about.
– Use encryption when you can, which should be in most cases, and certainly on your servers. Similar to password protection, if the data is lost or stolen and it is encrypted, then in most cases, you have little to worry about. Also, if you have compliance requirements, under most rules you will not have a reporting requirement if the data was encrypted.
– Use security tools like secure email and be smart about email and the Internet, when sending sensitive data, as mentioned earlier.
– Do you really need that app? There are a lot of apps that are seeded with malware, which is downloaded to your phone when you download the app. Many apps collect a lot of personal data about you which may then be available to the hackers. Do some research on apps before you actually download and start using them. And look

at the reviews and try and figure out whether you can trust the manufacturer.

— Be careful about whose network you're connecting to. Do you use public Wi-Fi, for example at coffee shops, airports, hotels, etc.? Hackers can easily set up a hotspot where public Wi-Fi is offered that many people will mindlessly connect to. For instance, I could set up a hotspot labeled "Free Starbucks Wi-Fi" and many people will connect to it without thinking twice about it. When they do, all their traffic will then go through my computer and I will be able to see everything, like emails, bank details, usernames, and passwords etc. So be very careful with public Wi-Fi and public networks you're connecting to. If you need Internet access consider tethering your phone to your computer either by using the USB charging cable or creating a password-protected hotspot on your phone that only you can use. If in a hotel remember to bring an Ethernet cable if you need to use the hotel Internet access. It does not create absolute security, but it is safer than the Wi-Fi.

— What data are you processing, collecting, storing? Be wary of what you have, how it is secured, and whether you need to keep it. If you don't need it, get rid of it. Also, hitting the delete key merely moves a pointer away from the data. It does not wipe or truly delete the data. In order to truly delete data consider using software, many are free, that will wipe the data multiple times thus making it more difficult to recover.

— Don't respond to unsolicited email, much of it is spam or scams. One important tip here is that you should not unsubscribe to unsolicited email right away because it may be the spammers trying to legitimize your email. When you unsubscribe you confirm that your email address is legitimate and active. If the email was from spammers you will most certainly end up on the spam list. If you feel the need unsubscribe, wait until you receive the email five or six times. After that chances are the email was likely legitimate, annoying, but legitimate. Another option is to just keep putting it into your junk folder.

— As we discussed earlier, avoid opening attachments unless you truly trust the sender. Even then, the sender may be trustworthy, like your mom, but she may have been duped and is now unknowingly forwarding the malware or virus to you and her friends. Many anti-virus programs will allow you to scan attachments before you open them. But, if the attachment contains a zero day attack (a zero day

vulnerability refers to a hole in software that is unknown to the vendor or malware or virus that is not known to the anti-virus companies yet), the anti-virus may not recognize it and mark it as clean. So, be careful, and do your due diligence.
- Do not fill out online forms in emails. As mentioned, compare the link in the email to the actual web address. We discussed looking at properties in emails to determine their legitimacy.
- Continuing with email security, as discussed, if you receive a social media request (LinkedIn, Facebook, other), or banking email, log directly into the official site. The link in the email and the request could be fake causing you to compromise your username and password. For banking, as mentioned, close all other windows on your computer before logging in since some secure sites could be compromised by other open windows. If you need to respond to or open attachments in an email, as another precaution, contact the business or individual that appeared to send it, if you are able, especially if you're not sure if they actually sent the email. Finally, if requested to act quickly or there is a sense of urgency, that's a good clue that the email might not be legit.
- Keep the location services on phones and mobile devices turned off. This will prevent the apps on your devices from tracking your location, sending you ads and reporting to others your location. In some circumstances a concern may exist that someone with access to one of your mobile devices placed an app on it to track you, e.g. a domestic violence scenario. Turing off location services will help to prevent this. Turning off location services doesn't affect 911. The police can still find you in an emergency, but it prevents all those apps from accessing your location and broadcasting it out.
- Use two-factor authentication. As discussed earlier this involves inputting a username and password, which is one factor, and then typically a one-time pin sent via text (sms messaging), to enter, then providing access. If your bank online, use social media or some other service and two-factor authentication is offered use it.
- Whether for banking, finances, human resources, or other processing of sensitive information, use a separate computer when you can. Try not to use the same computer that you use for email, surfing the Internet and social media, for sensitive and financial transactions.
- Finally, I recommend that you cover the camera and if you need to, cover the mic on computers and mobile devices if you are concerned

about what someone might see or hear. Hackers can certainly turn on your camera and the light won't necessarily illuminate indicating that it is on. Laptops and tablets are especially vulnerable simply because they are so mobile and brought to many locations. So, cover the camera with a piece of tape.

Passwords are huge issue because no one likes them and most find them inconvenient. Many people use very simple and easy-to-guess passwords making it easy for hackers. We have not discussed this much, but we do not just need to worry about hackers but also insider threats where we work. With that in mind, many incidents occur at work because people, in an effort not to have to remember multiple passwords or passwords changed frequently, write them down and place them close to their computer. Also, as mentioned, don't use the same password on multiple sites. If the hacker gets one password he then has access to multiple accounts. Don't use a word or two as your password. A dictionary attack will allow a hacker to quickly guess the password. A good password is at least, 12 or more characters, upper-case and lowercase letters, numbers and special characters.

Now, let's discuss vendors. Whether it is a cloud or any other vendor, security must be key and paramount. Read the contract, read the service legal agreement (SLA), and the Privacy statement. Make sure you know what the agreement says and that your data will be protected. Also, ask the vendor how they protect your data, if they've had a recent security audit, and if they're willing to share the results with you. Finally, ask the vendor if a breach or incident occurs on their network, will they notify you and how soon.

# CHAPTER 5

# Ethics

These next pages are specifically for CEOs and Management. Let's look at your ethical and fiduciary duties, responsibilities, and obligations.

Let's briefly review the responsibilities of corporate board members versus CEOs/executives to provide some perspective. In another book I cover board member responsibilities in more depth, but briefly the Board has a fiduciary duty to monitor risk and oversee the cyber program of the company. As CEOs/executives and Management, you are responsible for identifying risk to the company, creating and implementing the cyber security program, ensuring that the company meets its regulatory compliance requirements, as well as maintaining and keeping the Board informed about cyber security and other related risk in addition to the efforts taken to mitigate those risks. You are basically responsible for building, maintaining, and keeping the Board informed as to the state of security and actions taken.

CEOs/Executives/Management, you don't have the luxury of ignoring the cyber risk anymore and claiming, "Well, that is an IT issue. I don't have to worry about it; or, I'm not a technical person." This is your issue. Recently many corporate executives have resigned or lost their jobs over a massive breach, and it is only getting worse. This issue should cause you as much concern as the financial status and risk of the organization, as well as other risks that keep you up at night. I can't emphasize this enough, "You can't ignore it any-more!" You have a fiduciary and ethical duty to protect the company. If your company suffers a breach that goes public, the situation will go south very quickly, especially if you don't have a plan put in place. It is no longer enough to say you have a firewall, good pass-words, and one or more policies. You must implement and actively monitor the processes you have put in place. It is your responsibility to take an active role and manage security as you would any other process. Security is not a set-and-forget concept. Even if your company uses an IT company you need to be cognizant of what are they are doing, how they are securing information, and if something does happen how quickly you will be informed and you must have a plan ready to react quickly? Whether an IT company as a vendor or internal IT and security, as the CEO or an executive you must receive daily updates on the state of the network and security efforts. We are truly at war with the hackers and as the general you must have situational awareness. Your plan should include assignment of roles to those within the company and you should ensure everyone knows what to do, who to call and when. This will require exercising the plan you have put in place. Any plan that merely sits on the shelf is worthless. This typically occurs if you have a plan written for you and the attitude among the executives is that you have checked the block. Remember, security is not a set and forget concept. Make sure the plan and people are ready to go. After discovering a breach the only activities required are not merely technical, a forensic investigation to determine what happened and what was exposed. There are legal issues to address like breach notification and whether regulatory rules have been broken; messaging, such as what will be communicated to the public and by whom when the breach is exposed; proper collection of evidence; how the company's reputation will be protected; who will be in charge of various pieces of the incident response; what outside help is needed; is there insurance and what coverage is available; and a myriad of other issues.

Finally, beware of the SEC and the FTC and federal courts because they are beginning to hold companies responsible. Companies have been held liable for data breaches due to lack of security programs even when no damages were revealed or even claimed and no complaint from a potential victim. One of the best recent examples is the breach of RT Jones Capital Equities Management. They were fined by the SEC for having lackadaisical security. They suffered a breach and lost the personal information of about 100,000 clients. No potential victim has claimed identity theft as a result, and no lawsuit has been filed, yet. According to the private firm that did the investigation, there was no clear-cut evidence that data was actually compromised. Despite all of this, the SEC still fined RT Jones because they did not have policies in place and they did not have a plan. There were of security practices that had not been implemented either, most of which were basic[1]. On the surface it may appear that some of these government agencies are being a little heavy-handed, but on the other hand a lot of companies just aren't making the effort to do the basics when it comes to cyber security. I guess they believe they can just ignore it and not worry about it. At least until they get stung.

As the CEO, you don't have to be a cyber expert. You need a little bit of knowledge, surround yourself with experts who work for the company or outside support, and ask to receive regular reports about the company and the data security risk. You must be able to show that you have done your due diligence.

As the data breaches continue the number of class action lawsuit grows. Executives and management are beginning to be held accountable. As you recall, earlier we discussed some of the major breaches in the media. It's hard to keep up with them all, and it seems as though a major breach is announced in the news every week. As a result of the Target breach the CEO either resigned or was fired, as well as some in management, I believe, the CIO. Leadership is being held responsible by their companies when a breach occurs, and reputations sullied. For instance Sony, Target, and Home Depot. The class action lawsuit complaints are pointing directly at the activities, or lack thereof by management. In the Wyndham Hotels case, the complaint claimed that the Board failed to ensure that the company implemented adequate information security and procedures. In the Heartland Payment Systems case, shareholders sued directors for failing to protect the computer network and failing to meet their fiduciary duty. In the TJX case, shareholders sued claiming that directors did not meet their fiduciary duties of loyalty, good faith, and due care.

Along the lines of fiduciary duty and corporate judgement we should quickly review the Business Judgement Rule[2]. Here in the United States, this rule protects the decisions of the board of directors and management against second guessing by the courts as long as the decisions made are in good faith and are reasonable. If you are ignoring the cyber risk, have not implemented a cyber security program,

---

[1]"SEC Charges Investment Adviser with Failing to Adopt Proper Cybersecurity Policies and Procedures Prior To Breach," U.S. Security and Exchange Commission Press Release 2015-202, (Sept. 22, 2015), https://www.sec.gov/news/pressrelease/2015-202.html.
[2]"Business Judgement Rule," Legal Information Institute, Cornell University Law School, https://www.law.cornell.edu/wex/business_judgment_rule.

and do not have an active plan in place, these are not reasonable actions and decisions. This rule provides some protection for the decisions made, but they must be reasonable.

Finally, in order to show due care, CEOs must not make decisions in bad faith and must not fail to act where a known threat or risk exists i.e., data security risks. Bad faith would involve ignoring the risk, claiming you're not technical, or you don't understand this "stuff." If you feel like you need more knowledge to make a decision, then you better find the experts, get briefed, get you up to speed and get help with making that decision. If you have to hire outside support, just get it done, don't ignore it any longer.

# CHAPTER 6

## Conclusion

Bottom line, do your due diligence. Understand the data you have, how it is secured, who has access to it, where it resides, and what you will do if breached. There is a lot more information out there. This was just a brief overview so you need to continue to do your research and figure out what else you can do to keep things more secure.

### *Do You Feel Lucky?*

http://www.youtube.com/watch?v=u0-oinyjsk0

## *If not, get yourself a Plan!!*

So do you feel lucky? If so, then don't worry about it. If not, get yourself a plan.

# *Don't Be This Guy!!*

http://1rico.wordpress.com/2011/02/01/

But please, do not be this guy. Do not bury your head in the sand. If you suffer a breach and can't explain how you attempted to secure information and show that you had a data security plan, the risk, liability and reputation of the company goes through the roof.